ROOF DESIGN

daab

Introduction   4

Residential   8

Architectenbureau Paul de Ruiter | Villa Deys   10
Architecture Workshop/Koh Kitayama | Funabashi Minihousing Development   14
Architecture Workshop/Koh Kitayama | Iidabashi Apartments   18
Artec Architekten | B-B House   22
Atelier Tekuto | Lucky Drops   26
Brunete Fraccaroli | Barbecue Gourmet   32
Brunete Fraccaroli | Showroom   36
Curiosity | C-2   40
Delugan Meissl Associated Architects | Haus Ray 1   44
Enric Ruiz-Geli | Villa Bio   48
Griffin Enright Architects | Benedict Canyon Residence   52
Luca Gazzaniga Architetti | Cedrini House   56
Neutelings Riedijk | Housing Lakeshore Zone, Sphinxen   60
Neutelings Riedijk | Müllerpier, Block 3   64
Nolaster | OS House   68
Nurmela-Raimoranta-Tasa | Moby Dick House   74
Odden Rodrigues Architects | Ozone Parade House   78
Original Vision Limited/Adrian McCarroll | Samsara   82
Salmela | Emerson Sauna   86
Shuhei Endo | Rooftecture S   90
Shuhei Endo | Springtecture B   94
Slade Architecture, Mass Studies | Pixel House   100
Stefan Sterf Architekten | Sunny Side Up   104
Steven Holl Architects | Turbulence House   108

Corporative   112

Architecture Workshop Ltd. | Peregrine Winery   114
Arquitectonica | Sarasota Herald Tribune Media Headquarters   118
Carlos Alberto Silva Zaldívar | Amayna Winery   124
Drozdov & Partners | "Yaske" Sushi Bar   128
Future Systems | Selfridges   134
Gehry Partners | Hotel Marqués de Riscal, The Luxury Collection   138
Germán del Sol | Remota Hotel   144
Grimshaw | Frankfurt Trade Fair Hall   148
Ingenhoven Architekten | Peek & Cloppenburg Department Store (Chemnitz)   154
Ingenhoven Architekten | Peek & Cloppenburg Department Store (Lübeck)   158
Jun Itami | Podo Hotel   162
Kiessler & Partner Architekten | K21 Düsseldorf   166
Machné Architekten | Sarrasine   170
Marc Prosman Architecten | Horse Barn   174
Massimiliano Fuksas | Europark 2   178
Massimiliano Fuksas, Doriana O. Mandrelli | New Trade Fair Milan   182
Nande Korpnik | Maksimilijan   190
ONL – Oosterhuis-Lénárd | Cockpit Building   194
Richard Rogers Partnership, Alonso-Balaguer y Arquitectos Asociados | Hesperia Tower Hotel   202

RKW Architektur & Städtebau | Audi Electronic Center 208
RKW Architektur & Städtebau | House of the Medical Fraternity 212
Sauerbruch Hutton Architects | Experimental Factory 216
Steven Holl Architects | Whitney Water Purification Facility and Park 220

Cultural 224

EEA – Frick van Egeraat Associated Architects | Popstage Mezz Breda 226
Fasch & Fuchs | Kindermuseum 230
Gehry Partners | Marta Museum 234
Griffin Enright Architects | The John Thomas Dye School 238
Jarmund & Vigsnæs | Svalbard Science Centre 242
John Portman & Associates | Charles H. Jones Building at Macon State College 248
John Portman & Associates | Gwinnett University Center 252
Josep Llinàs i Carmona | Jaume Fuster Public Library 256
Jun Itami | Water Art Museum 262
Paulo David | Casa das Mudas Art Center 266
Peter Cook, Coulin Fournier | Art Museum Graz 270
Plan 01 Architects | Historical Museum of Vendée 274
Richard Rogers Partnership/Ivan Harbour | Minami Yamashiro Primary School 278
Úrsula Heredia, Ramón Velasco | Roman Theatre 282

Other facilities 286

EMBT – Enric Miralles & Benedetta Tagliabue | Scottish Parliament 288
EMBT – Enric Miralles & Benedetta Tagliabue | Sta. Caterina Market 296
Emmanuel Combarel Dominique Marrec Architectes | Lycée La Tourelle Gymnasium 300
Estudio Lamela Arquitectos, Richard Rogers Partnership | New Aerial Terminal at Madrid-Barajas Airport 306
Fxfowle Architects | Stillwell Avenue Terminal 312
GMP Architekten | Berlin Central Station 316
Grimshaw | Southern Cross Station 324
Harmer Architecture | Gatehouse Mausoleum, Melbourne General Cemetery 332
Josep Miàs i Gifre | Golf Club Fontanals 336
Justo García Rubio | Bus Station 342
Kisho Kurokawa Architect & Associates | Oita Main Stadium 348
Monika Gora | The Glass Bubble 352
Pittino & Other Architekturbüro | Public Bath Wellenbad Gleisdorf 358
Renzo Piano Building Workshop | Padre Pio Pilgrimage Church 362
Smarch, Mathys & Stücheli Architekten | New Apostolic Church 366
Smarch, Mathys & Stücheli Architekten | Wave of Bern 372
Spacelab | Great Ormond Street Hospital 380
Vito Acconci, Purpur Architektur | Mur Insel 384
Wilkinson Eyre Architects | Davies Alpine House 390

Index 394
Imprint 400

The world seen from high above, the nocturnal skyline of a city or, simply the recovery of a forgotten part of the home, are just three ideas that allude directly or indirectly to the highest part of a building. This is an introduction to a publication, which shows us that an attractively designed roof continues to be of great importance in today's architecture.

The increase in population density and the price of land during the last century is why living on top of a building has become a symbol of personal and material wealth, since this position gained privacy and distance from the increasingly crowded streets. With time, «rooftops» have also symbolized a reaffirmation of a new lifestyle —an extension of the livable surface area and exclusive enjoyment of an area traditionally unused—. This complements and reinforces its basic function, that of an architectural crown for the building and creating a new area for living in or as a workplace. Architects, designers and town planners have seen in this final section of a building, their last chance to let their fantasies run free and to dramatically shape the cities' skylines with extensions, attics with views and unique rooftops.

And what does the future hold in store for the design of this increasingly valued part of our homes? In the 1930s, Dischinger, Finsterwalder and Bauersfeld set the guidelines so that emerging technology would convert rooftops into a cultural reference, but little would they have imagined that the relentless advance in construction engineering would not only achieve functional and technical success (the secret desire to defy gravity) but also an aesthetical one. So, this collection of relevant rooftops —from minimalist to maximilist, lightweight to magnificent— can maybe help us to understand that the dream of any architect still has a wide margin for expression particularly when their projects get closer to the skies.

Die Welt von oben betrachtet, die nächtliche Silhouette einer Stadt oder einfach nur die Renovierung eines Gebäudeteils, der im Laufe der Geschichte immer mehr an Bedeutung verlor, das sind nur drei der Ideen, die direkt oder indirekt die Gestaltung des obersten Teil eines Gebäudes beeinflussen. Dieser Band dient lediglich als eine Art Einführung, und trotzdem beweist er, dass die attraktive Gestaltung eines Daches der Architektur der Gegenwart einen zusätzlichen Wert gibt.

Die Erhöhung der Bevölkerungsdichte und der Grundstückspreise im vergangenen Jahrhundert sind die Gründe dafür, dass das Leben im obersten Stockwerk zu einem Symbol für persönlichen und materiellen Reichtum geworden ist. Oben gewinnt man an Privatsphäre und Distanz zu den immer volleren Straßen. Im Laufe der Zeit haben sich Dachwohnungen auch zu einer Art Symbol für einen neuen Lebensstil entwickelt. Durch den Dachausbau wurde nicht nur mehr Wohnfläche zur Verfügung gestellt, sondern man begann auch einen Teil des Hauses zu nutzen und genießen, der in der Vergangenheit eher unbeliebt war, und so ergänzte und erweiterte man die grundlegende Funktion des Daches, nämlich ein Gebäude architektonisch abzuschließen, und schuf einen neuen Bereich zum Wohnen und Arbeiten. Außerdem haben die Architekten, Innenarchitekten und Stadtplaner in diesen Dachgeschossen den Ort entdeckt, an dem sie ihrer Phantasie freien Lauf lassen und auf großzügige Weise die Silhouette der Stadt mit Ausbauten, Dachwohnungen mit Ausblick und einzigartigen Dächern gestalten können.

Und welche Zukunft kann man bei der Gestaltung dieses Teils unserer Gebäude erwarten, der immer mehr an Wert gewinnt? In den Dreißigerjahren des vergangenen Jahrhunderts zeigten Konstrukteure wie Dischinger, Finsterwalder und Bauersfeld, wie die neue Technologie aus Dächern eine kulturelle Referenz machen konnte. Was sie sich zu jener Zeit jedoch wohl kaum vorstellen konnten, war es, dass der unaufhörliche Fortschritt der Konstruktionstechnik nicht nur technische und funktionelle Verbesserungen suchen sollte, denn irgendwie wünschte man ja immer, der Schwerkraft zu trotzen, sondern dass auch ästhetische Ziele stark an Bedeutung gewinnen würden. Man muss verstehen, dass es der Traum eines jeden Architekten ist, ein ganz besonderes Dach zu konstruieren, sei es minimalistisch oder maximalistisch, leicht oder pompös, denn an diesem Teil des Bauwerks, das dem Himmel am nächsten ist, finden sie auch die größte Freiheit, um sich auszudrücken.

El mundo visto desde las alturas, el perfil nocturno de una ciudad o, simplemente, la recuperación de una parte de la vivienda históricamente olvidada, son sólo tres ideas que aluden directa o indirectamente al diseño de la parte más alta de un edificio. En pocas palabras, a lo largo de esta publicación se podrá comprobar que el diseño atractivo de un tejado sigue sumando más que restando en el cómputo global de la arquitectura de nuestros días.

El aumento de la densidad demográfica y el precio de los solares durante el siglo pasado explica que vivir en lo alto de las viviendas se haya convertido en un símbolo de riqueza personal y material, ya que de esa forma se ganaba privacidad y distancia respecto a un plano terrestre cada vez más concurrido. Con el tiempo los «rooftops» también han simbolizado una reafirmación de un nuevo estilo de vida —ampliación de la superficie habitable así como disfrute exclusivo de una parte tradicionalmente relegada—, que complementa y refuerza su función básica, la de culminar arquitectónicamente el inmueble y habilitar una nueva zona como vivienda o lugar de trabajo. Además, los arquitectos, diseñadores y urbanistas han visto en la parte final de las viviendas el último filón para dar rienda suelta a su fantasía y esculpir generosamente el perfil de sus ciudades con extensiones, áticos con vistas, tejados y cubiertas singulares.

¿Y qué futuro se espera del diseño de esta parte cada vez más valorada de nuestras viviendas? Si bien en los años treinta del siglo pasado, Dischinger, Finsterwalder y Bauersfeld marcaron las pautas para que la tecnología emergente convirtiera los tejados en referencia cultural, pocos se podían imaginar que el avance ininterrumpido de la ingeniería de la construcción acabase explicando que en la actualidad no sólo se busque el logro funcional y técnico (ese anhelo secreto de desafiar la gravedad), sino la recreación estética. Por ello, esta colección de techumbres relevantes —de minimalistas a maximalistas; de ligeras a ostentosas— quizá nos ayude a entender que el sueño de cualquier arquitecto sigue teniendo un amplio margen de expresión precisamente en la parte de sus obras más cercana al cielo.

Le monde, observé depuis les hauteurs, le profil nocturne d'une ville ou, simplement, la récupération d'un élément architectonique longtemps oublié par l'histoire, sont trois simples idées faisant allusion – directement ou indirectement – au design de la partie la plus élevée d'un édifice. Au fil de cet ouvrage et en peu de mots, l'idée s'impose, de qu'une conception attrayante de toit augmente clairement la qualité globale de l'architecture contemporaine.

La croissance de la densité démographique et les prix de l'immobilier au cours du siècle passé expliquent que la vie sous les toits se soit convertie en un symbole de richesse personnelle et matérielle, représentant la forme idéale de jouir d'une intimité et d'une certaine distance avec des rues toujours plus fréquentées. En agrandissant la surface habitable et en réhabilitant un nouvelle zone en demeure ou espace de travail tout en bénéficiant de l'exclusivité de cet étage traditionnellement laissé pour compte, les « rooftops » en sont arrivés, entre temps, à symboliser un nouveau style de vie qui parachève la fonction essentielle de cette partie du bâtiment : celle d'apogée architecturale de l'immeuble.

Les architectes, créateurs et urbanistes ont su déceler dans la partie culminante des bâtiments une ultime possibilité de donner libre cours à leur créativité et de remodeler sans parcimonie le profil de leurs villes au grés d'extensions, de lofts avec vue, de toits et de revêtements singuliers.

Et dans le futur, qu'attendons-nous du design de cet élément toujours plus valorisé de nos demeures ? Si, dans les années 1930, Dischinger, Finsterwalder et Bauersfeld ont donné le ton afin que la technologie émergente convertisse les toits en référence culturelle, bien peu néanmoins auraient pu imaginer que le progrès ininterrompu de l'ingénierie du bâtiment finirait par permettre non seulement la poursuite de la réussite fonctionnelle et technique (ce secret désir de défier la gravité) mais aussi de la création esthétique novatrice. De ce fait, cette collection de toitures représentatives – des plus minimalistes aux maximalistes, des graciles aux plus somptueuses – nous aidera peut être à comprendre que, précisément dans la partie de son œuvre la plus proche du ciel, tout architecte dispose encore d'une ample marge d'expression pour ses rêves.

Il mondo visto dall'alto, lo skyline notturno di una città o, semplicemente, il recupero di una parte della casa storicamente dimenticata, sono solo tre idee che alludono, in modo diretto o indiretto, alla progettazione della parte più alta di un edificio. In breve, nell'ambito di questa pubblicazione si metterà in luce come la buona progettazione di un tetto sia un valore aggiunto nel computo globale dell'architettura dei nostri giorni.

L'aumento della densità demografica e del prezzo dei terreni edificabili, durante il secolo scorso, è la ragione per cui vivere nella parte più alta di un edificio è diventato un simbolo di ricchezza personale e materiale. Infatti, questa posizione permetteva di godere di maggior privacy e distanza rispetto al livello del suolo che si faceva sempre più affollato. Con il tempo, i «rooftops» hanno cominciato a rappresentare anche l'affermazione di un nuovo stile di vita —aumento della superficie abitabile e godimento esclusivo di una parte tradizionalmente relegata—, che completa e rafforza la loro funzione fondamentale: coronare architettonicamente l'immobile e abilitare una nuova zona ad uso residenziale o come luogo di lavoro. Inoltre, architetti, designer e urbanisti hanno visto nella parte più alta degli edifici residenziali l'ultimo filone per dare briglia sciolta alla loro fantasia e scolpire generosamente lo skyline delle loro città con ampliamenti, attici con vista, tetti e coperture singolari.

E quale futuro c'è da aspettarsi dalla progettazione di questa parte sempre più valorizzata delle nostre case? Anche se, durante gli anni 30 del secolo scorso, Dischinger, Finsterwalder e Bauersfeld dettarono le linee guida per far sì che la tecnologia emergente trasformasse i tetti in un punto di riferimento culturale, pochi si sarebbero immaginati che il progresso ininterrotto dell'ingegneria edile avrebbe finito per spiegare l'attuale ricerca non solo dell'efficacia funzionale e tecnica (l'anelo segreto a sfidare la gravità), ma anche del compiacimento estetico. Per questa ragione, è probabile che la presente raccolta di tetti rilevanti —minimalisti e massimalisti; leggeri e pomposi— possa aiutarci a capire come il sogno di qualsiasi architetto continui ad avere un ampio margine d'espressione proprio nella parte delle sue opere più vicina al cielo.

RESIDENTIAL

ARCHITECTENBUREAU PAUL DE RUITER | AMSTERDAM
VILLA DEYS
Rhenen, The Netherlands | 2002

ARCHITECTURE WORKSHOP/KOH KITAYAMA | TOKYO
FUNABASHI MINIHOUSING DEVELOPMENT
Funabashi, Japan | 2003

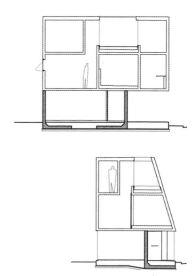

ARCHITECTURE WORKSHOP/KOH KITAYAMA | TOKYO
IIDABASHI APARTMENTS
Wakamiya-cho, Japan | 2002

ARTEC ARCHITEKTEN | VIENNA
B-B HOUSE
Bocksdorf, Austria | 2005

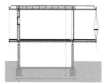

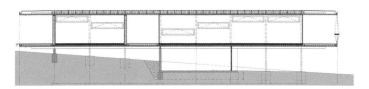

ATELIER TEKUTO | TOKYO
LUCKY DROPS
Tokyo, Japan | 2005

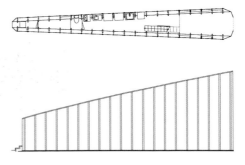

BRUNETE FRACCAROLI | SÃO PAULO

BARBECUE GOURMET
São Paulo, Brazil | 2004

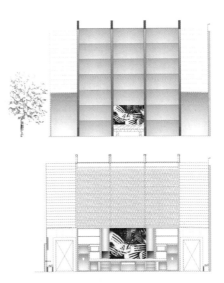

BRUNETE FRACCAROLI | SÃO PAULO
SHOWROOM
São Paulo, Brazil | 2004

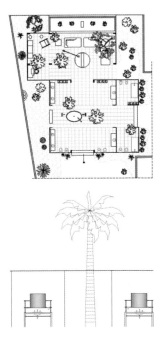

CURIOSITY | TOKYO
C-2
Yamanashi, Japan | 2006

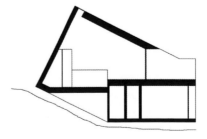

DELUGAN MEISSL ASSOCIATED ARCHITECTS | VIENNA
HAUS RAY 1
Vienna, Austria | 2003

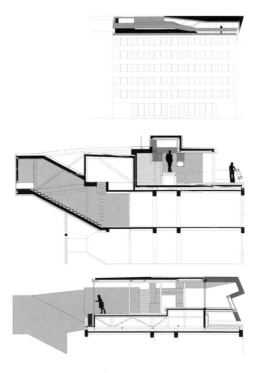

ENRIC RUIZ-GELI | BARCELONA
VILLA BIO
Hostalets de Llers, Spain | 2005

GRIFFIN ENRIGHT ARCHITECTS | LOS ANGELES
BENEDICT CANYON RESIDENCE
Beverly Hills, USA | 2005

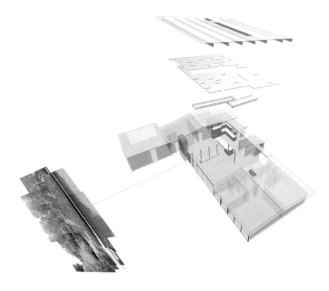

LUCA GAZZANIGA ARCHITETTI | LUGANO
CEDRINI HOUSE
Muzzano, Italy | 2004

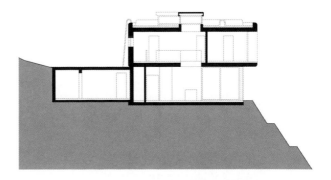

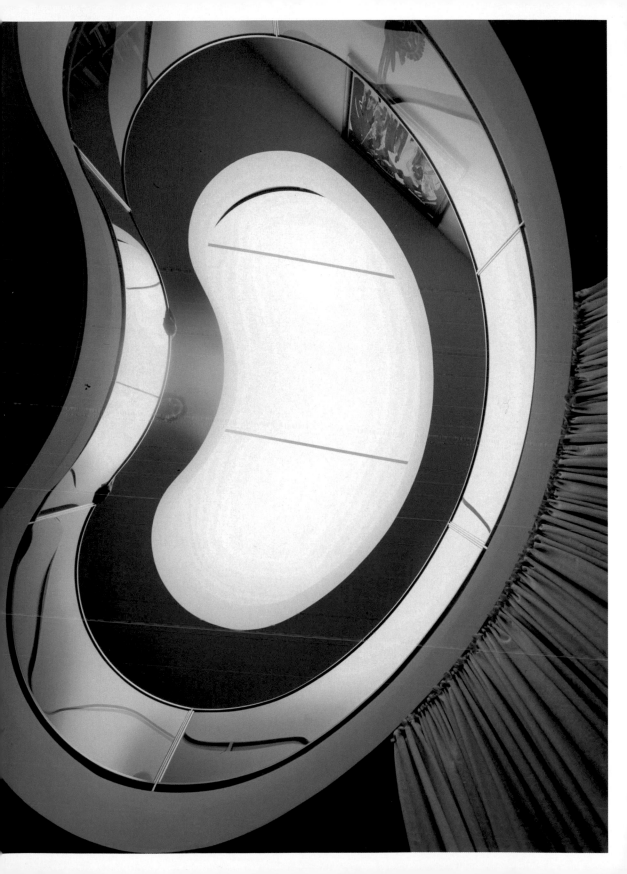

NEUTELINGS RIEDIJK | ROTTERDAM
HOUSING LAKESHORE ZONE, SPHINXEN
Huizen, The Netherlands | 2003

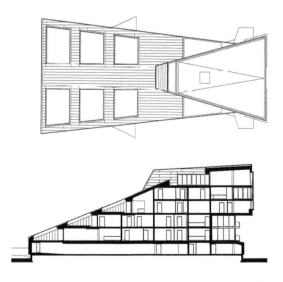

NEUTELINGS RIEDIJK | ROTTERDAM
MÜLLERPIER, BLOCK 3
Rotterdam, The Netherlands | 2003

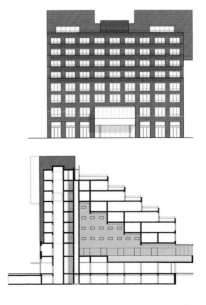

NOLASTER | MADRID
OS HOUSE
Loredo, Spain | 2005

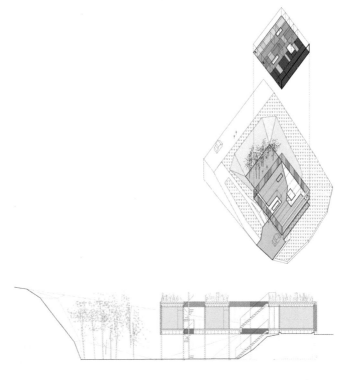

NURMELA-RAIMORANTA-TASA | HELSINKI
MOBY DICK HOUSE
Espoo, Finland | 2003

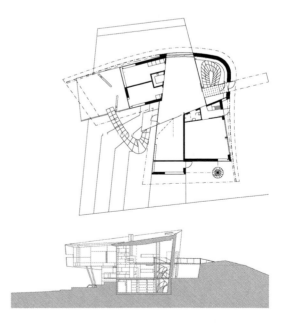

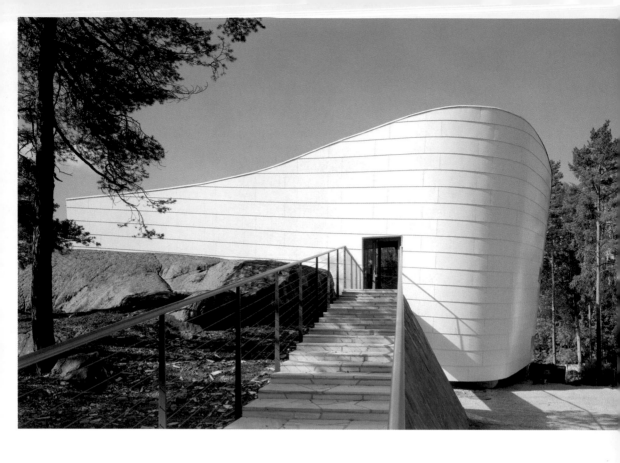

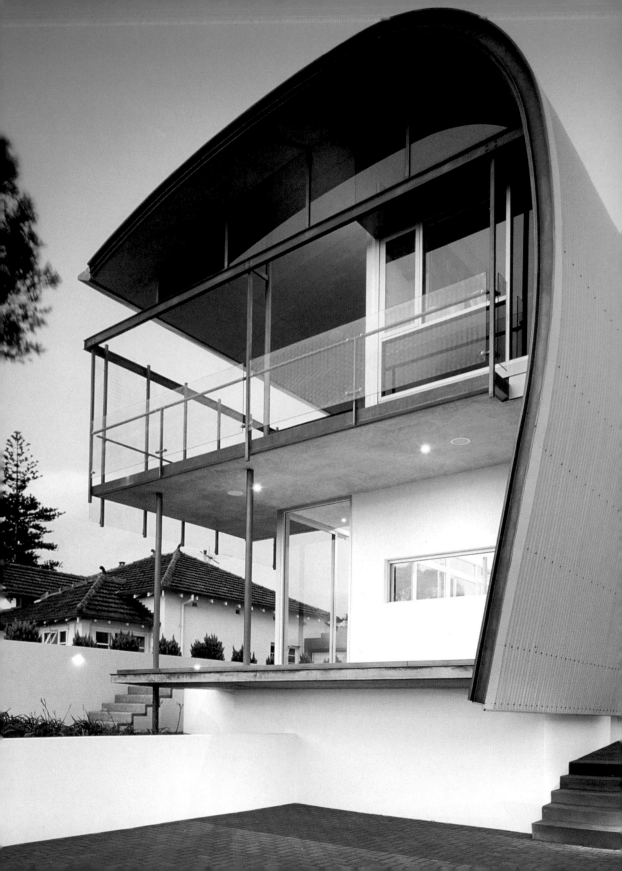

ODDEN RODRIGUES ARCHITECTS | CLAREMONT
OZONE PARADE HOUSE
Perth, Australia | 2002

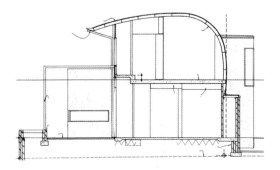

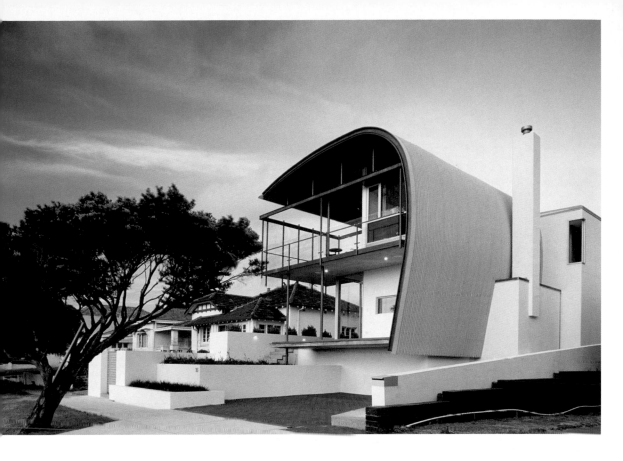

ORIGINAL VISION LIMITED/ADRIAN McCARROLL | HONG KONG
SAMSARA
Phuket, Thailand | 2004

SHUHEI ENDO | OSAKA
ROOFTECTURE S
Hyogo, Japan | 2005

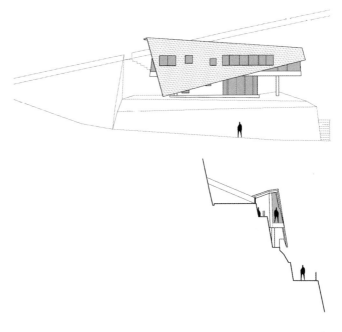

SHUHEI ENDO | OSAKA
SPRINGTECTURE B
Shiga, Japan | 2002

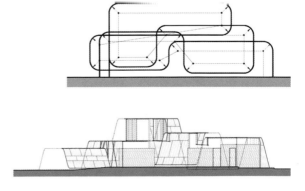

SLADE ARCHITECTURE | NEW YORK
MASS STUDIES | SEOUL
PIXEL HOUSE
Heyri, South Korea | 2001

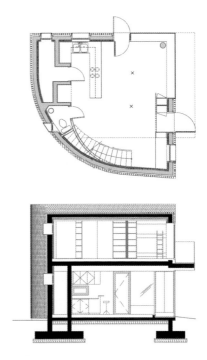

STEFAN STERF ARCHITEKTEN | BERLIN
SUNNY SIDE UP
Berlin, Germany | 2005

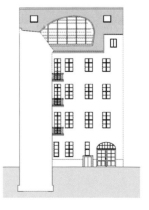

STEVEN HOLL ARCHITECTS | NEW YORK
TURBULENCE HOUSE
Abiqui, New Mexico, USA | 2004

CORPORATIVE

ARCHITECTURE WORKSHOP LTD. | WELLINGTON
PEREGRINE WINERY
Gibbston Valley, Queenstown, New Zealand | 2005

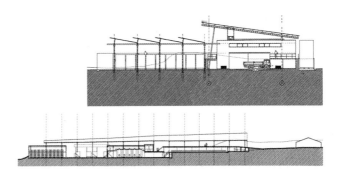

ARQUITECTONICA | MIAMI
SARASOTA HERALD TRIBUNE MEDIA HEADQUARTERS
Sarasota, USA | 2005

CARLOS ALBERTO SILVA ZALDÍVAR | SANTIAGO DE CHILE
AMAYNA WINERY
San Antonio, 5.ª Región, Chile | 2004

DROZDOV & PARTNERS | KHARKOV
"YASKE" SUSHI BAR
Kharkov, Ukraine | 2004

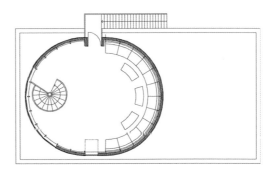

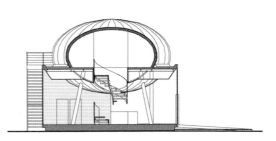

FUTURE SYSTEMS | **LONDON**
SELFRIDGES
Birmingham, UK | 2003

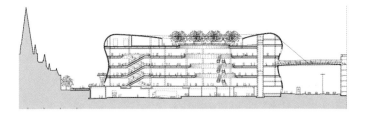

GEHRY PARTNERS | LOS ANGELES
HOTEL MARQUÉS DE RISCAL, THE LUXURY COLLECTION
Elciego, Spain | 2006

GERMÁN DEL SOL | **SANTIAGO DE CHILE**
REMOTA HOTEL
Magallanes, Chile | 2006

GRIMSHAW | LONDON
FRANKFURT TRADE FAIR HALL
Frankfurt, Germany | 2001

INGENHOVEN ARCHITEKTEN | DÜSSELDORF
PEEK & CLOPPENBURG DEPARTMENT STORE
Chemnitz, Germany | 2003

INGENHOVEN ARCHITEKTEN | DÜSSELDORF
PEEK & CLOPPENBURG DEPARTMENT STORE
Lübeck, Germany | 2005

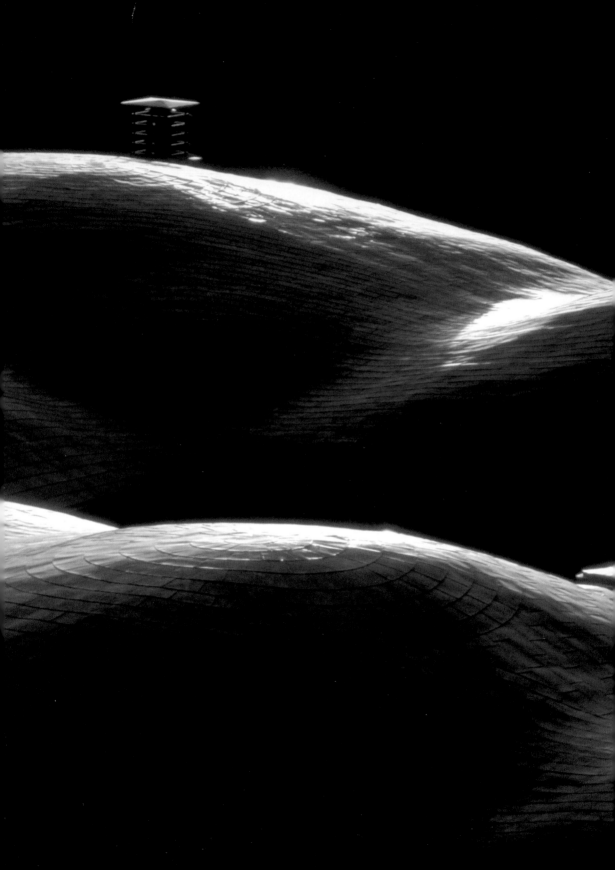

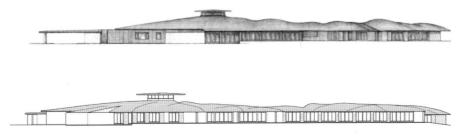

KIESSLER & PARTNER ARCHITEKTEN | MUNICH
K21 DÜSSELDORF
Düsseldorf, Germany | 2002

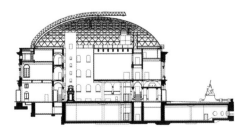

MACHNÉ ARCHITEKTEN | INNSBRUCK
SARRASINE
Matrei, Austria | 2004

MARC PROSMAN ARCHITECTEN | AMSTERDAM
HORSE BARN
Putten, The Netherlands | 2005

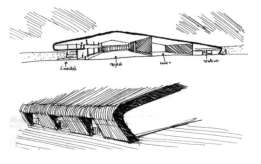

MASSIMILIANO FUKSAS | **ROME**
EUROPARK 2
Salzburg, Austria | 2003

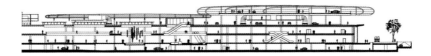

MASSIMILIANO FUKSAS, DORIANA O. MANDRELLI | ROME
NEW TRADE FAIR MILAN
Milan, Italy | 2005

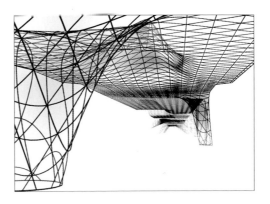

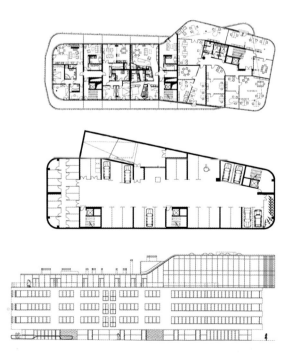

ONL — GOOSTERHUIS-LÉNÁRD | ROTTERDAM
COCKPIT BUILDING
Utrecht, The Netherlands | 2005

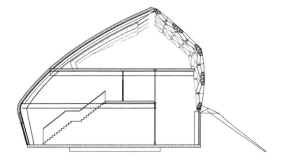

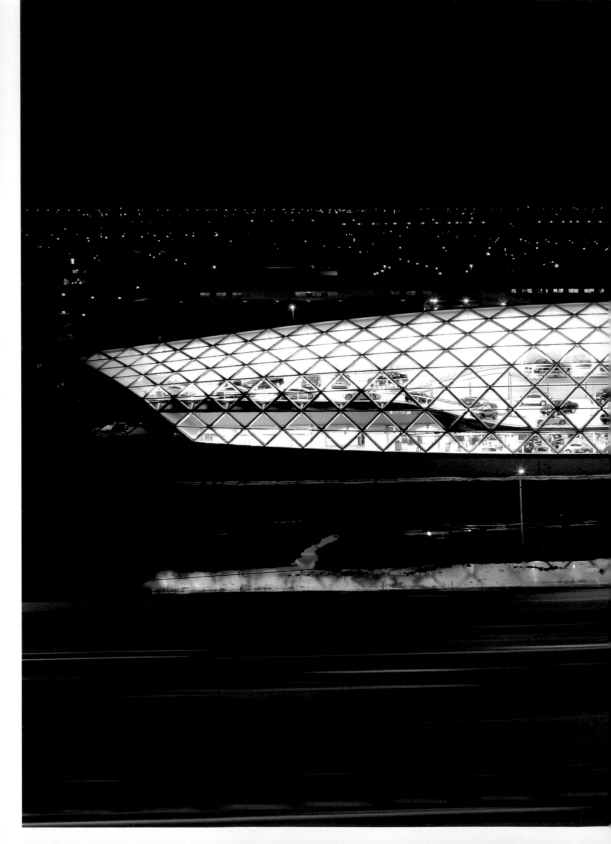

RICHARD ROGERS PARTNERSHIP | LONDON
ALONSO-BALAGUER Y ARQUITECTOS ASOCIADOS | BARCELONA
HESPERIA TOWER HOTEL
L'Hospitalet de Llobregat, Spain | 2006

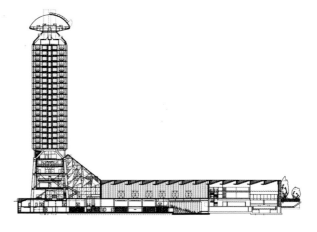

RKW ARCHITEKTUR & STÄDTEBAU | DÜSSELDORF
AUDI ELECTRONIC CENTER
Ingolstadt, Germany | 2003

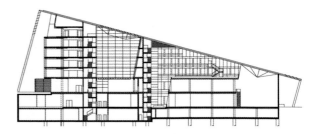

RKW ARCHITEKTUR & STÄDTEBAU | DÜSSELDORF
HOUSE OF THE MEDICAL FRATERNITY
Düsseldorf, Germany | 2003

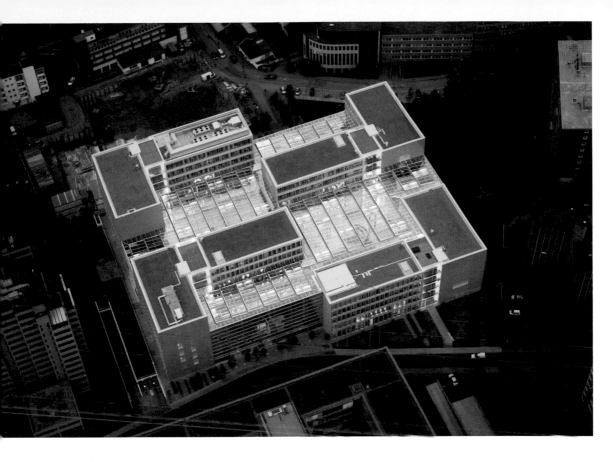

SAUERBRUCH HUTTON ARCHITECTS | BERLIN
EXPERIMENTAL FACTORY
Magdeburg, Germany | 2001

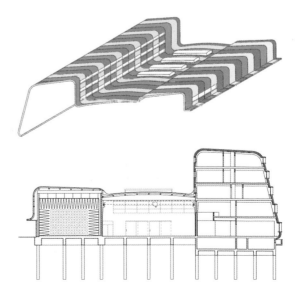

STEVEN HOLL ARCHITECTS | NEW YORK
WHITNEY WATER PURIFICATION FACILITY AND PARK
Connecticut, USA | 2005

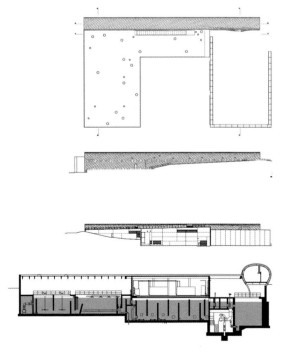

CULTURAL

EEA — ERICK VAN EGERAAT ASSOCIATED ARCHITECTS | ROTTERDAM
POPSTAGE MEZZ BREDA
Breda, The Netherlands | 2002

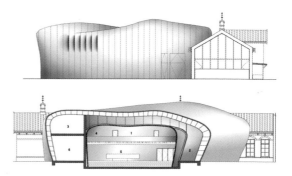

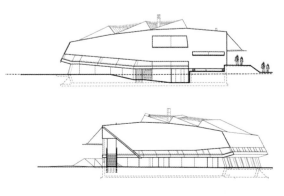

GEHRY PARTNERS | **LOS ANGELES**
MARTA MUSEUM
Herford, Germany | 2005

GRIFFIN ENRIGHT ARCHITECTS | LOS ANGELES
THE JOHN THOMAS DYE SCHOOL
Los Angeles, USA | 2004

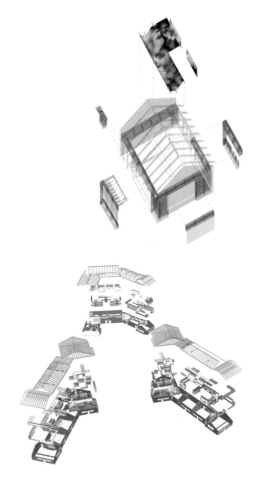

JARMUND & VIGSNÆS | OSLO
SVALBARD SCIENCE CENTRE
Longyearbyen, Svalbard | 2005

JOHN PORTMAN & ASSOCIATES | ATLANTA
CHARLES H. JONES BUILDING AT MACON STATE COLLEGE
Macon, Georgia, USA | 2004

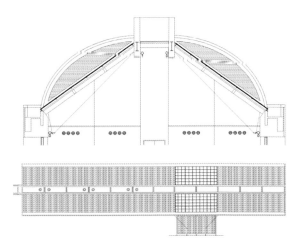

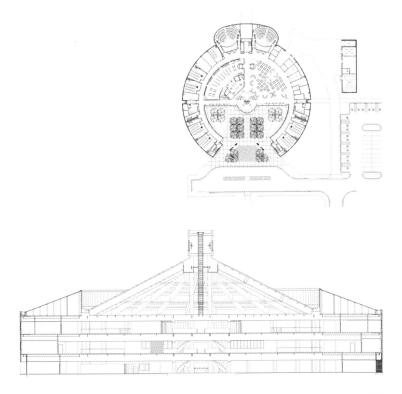

JOSEP LLINÀS I CARMONA | BARCELONA
JAUME FUSTER PUBLIC LIBRARY
Barcelona, Spain | 2005

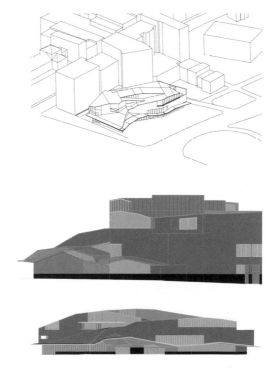

JUN ITAMI | TOKYO
WATER ART MUSEUM
Cheju Island, South Korea | 2005

PAULO DAVID | FUNCHAL
CASA DAS MUDAS ART CENTER
Calheta, Portugal | 2004

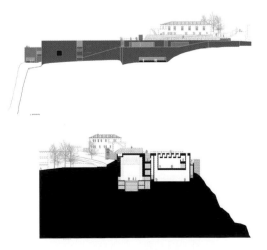

PETER COOK, COULIN FOURNIER | LONDON
ART MUSEUM GRAZ
Graz, Austria | 2003

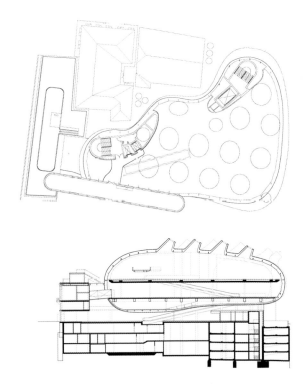

PLAN 01 ARCHITECTS | PARIS
HISTORICAL MUSEUM OF VENDÉE
Les Lucs-sur-Boulogne, France | 2006

RICHARD ROGERS PARTNERSHIP / IVAN HARBOUR | LONDON
MINAMI YAMASHIRO PRIMARY SCHOOL
Kyoto, Japan | 2003

ÚRSULA HEREDIA, RAMÓN VELASCO | ZARAGOZA
ROMAN THEATRE
Zaragoza, Spain | 2003

EMBT — ENRIC MIRALLES & BENEDETTA TAGLIABUE | BARCELONA
SCOTTISH PARLIAMENT
Edinburgh, UK | 2004

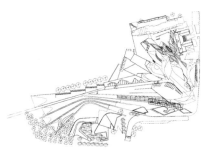

EMBT — ENRIC MIRALLES & BENEDETTA TAGLIABUE | BARCELONA
STA. CATERINA MARKET
Barcelona, Spain | 2005

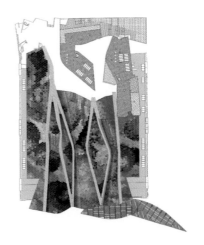

EMMANUEL COMBAREL DOMINIQUE MARREC ARCHITECTES | PARIS
LYCÉE LA TOURELLE GYMNASIUM
Sarcelles, France | 2005

ESTUDIO LAMELA ARQUITECTOS | MADRID
RICHARD ROGERS PARTNERSHIP | LONDON
NEW AERIAL TERMINAL AT MADRID-BARAJAS AIRPORT
Madrid, Spain | 2006

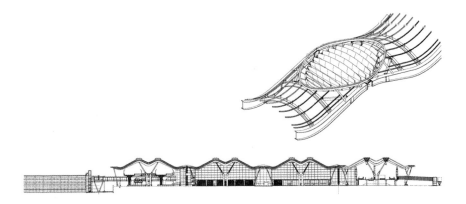

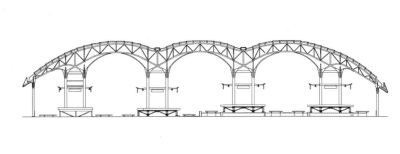

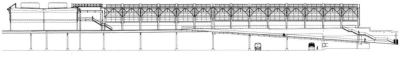

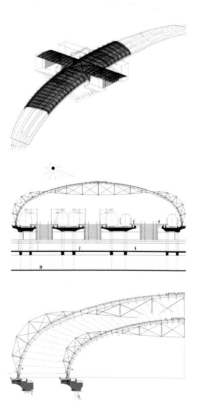

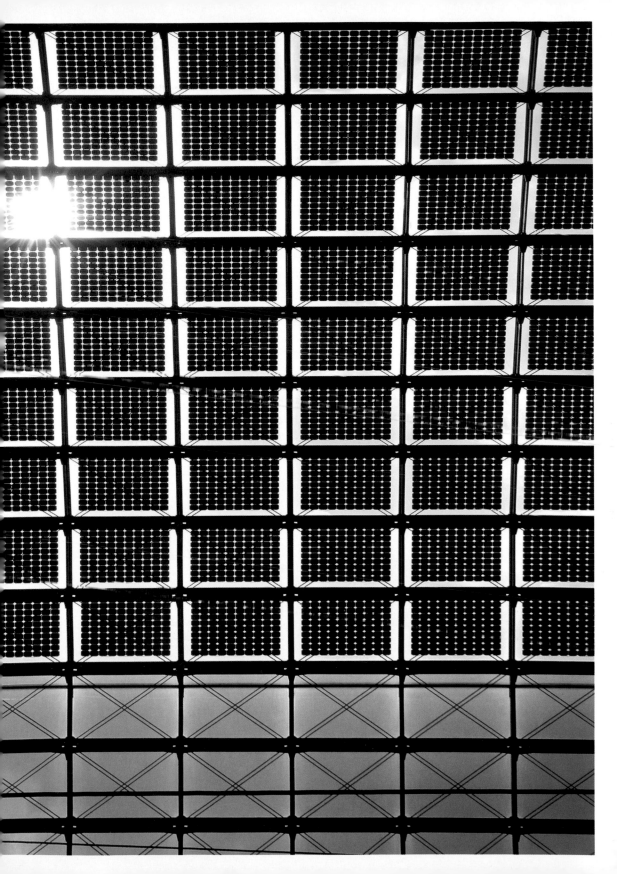

GRIMSHAW | LONDON
SOUTHERN CROSS STATION
Melbourne, Australia | 2006

HARMER ARCHITECTURE | VICTORIA
GATEHOUSE MAUSOLEUM, MELBOURNE GENERAL CEMETERY
Melbourne, Australia | 2005

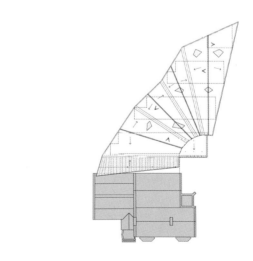

JOSEP MIÀS GIFRE | **BARCELONA**
GOLF CLUB FONTANALS
Fontanals de Cerdanya, Spain | 2004

JUSTO GARCÍA RUBIO | CÁCERES
BUS STATION
Casar de Cáceres, Spain | 2006

KISHO KUROKAWA ARCHITECT & ASSOCIATES | TOKYO
OITA MAIN STADIUM
Oita, Japan | 2001

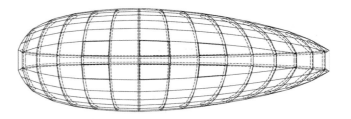

PITTINO & ORTNER ARCHITEKTURBÜRO | DEUTSCHLANDSBERG
PUBLIC BATH WELI ENBAD GLEISDORF
Gleisdorf, Germany | 2004

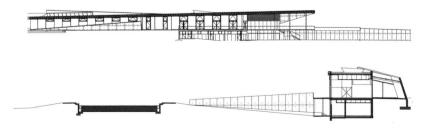

RENZO PIANO BUILDING WORKSHOP | GENOA
PADRE PIO PILGRIMAGE CHURCH
S. Giovanni Rotondo, Italy | 2004

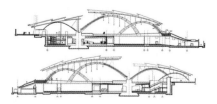

SMARCH, MATHYS & STÜCHELI ARCHITEKTEN | BERN
NEW APOSTOLIC CHURCH
Zuchwil, Switzerland | 2005

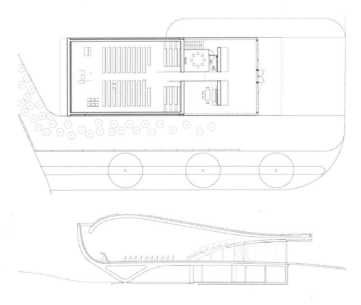

SMARCH, MATHYS & STÜCHELI ARCHITEKTEN | BERN
WAVE OF BERN
Bern, Switzerland | 2005

SPACELAB | LONDON
GREAT ORMOND STREET HOSPITAL
London, UK | 2004

VITO ACCONCI | NEW YORK
PURPUR ARCHITEKTUR | GRAZ
MUR INSEL
Graz, Austria | 2003

WILKINSON EYRE ARCHITECTS | LONDON
DAVIES ALPINE HOUSE
Richmond, UK | 2006

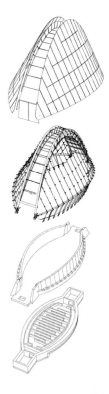

Alonso-Balaguer y Arquitectos Asociados
C/Bac de Roda 40
08019 Barcelona, Spain
P +34 93 303 41 60
F +34 93 303 41 61
estudi@alonsobalaguer.com
www.alonsobalaguer.com
Hesperia Tower Hotel
Photos: © David Cardelus, Pedro Pegenaute

Architectenbureau Paul de Ruiter b.v.
Leidsestraat 8-10
NL-1017 PA Amsterdam, The Netherlands
P +31 20 626 3244
F +31 20 623 7002
info@paulderuiter.nl
www.paulderuiter.nl
Villa Deys
Photos: © Rien van Rijthoven

Architecture Workshop/Koh Kitayama
2-14-21 BF Motoazabu, Minato
106-0046 Tokyo, Japan
P +81 3 5449 8337
F +81 3 5449 4822
aws@archws.com
www.archws.com
Funabashi Minihousing Development
Photos: © Daici Ano
Iidabashi Apartments
Photos: © Daici Ano

Architecture Workshop Ltd.
PO box 9572
Wellington, New Zealand
email@archwksp.co.nz
www.archwksp.co.nz
Peregrine Winery
Photos: © Patrick Reynolds

Arquitectonica
801 Brickell Avenue Suite 1100
Miami, FL 33131, USA
P +1 30 5372 1812
F +1 30 5372 1175
www.arquitectonica.com
Sarasota Herald Tribune Media Headquarters
Photos: © Norman McGrath

Artec Architekten
Am Hundsturm 5
A-1050 Vienna, Austria
P +43 1586 8670
F +43 1586 3910
www.artec-architekten.at
B-B House
Photos: © Paul Ott

Atelier Tekuto
301, 6-15-16, Honkomagome, Bunkyo-ku
113-0021, Tokyo, Japan
P +81 3 5940 2770
F +81 3 5940 2780
info@tekuto.com
www.tekuto.com
Lucky Drops
Photos: © Makoto Yoshida

Brunete Fraccaroli
Rua Guarará 261, 7.º andar jd. Paulista
SP 01425-001 São Paulo, Brazil
P +55 11 3885 8309
www.brunetefraccaroli.com.br
Barbecue Gourmet
Photos: © Rômulo Fialdini
Showroom
Photos: © Tuca Reinés

Carlos Alberto Silva Zaldívar
Don Carlos 3263, Las Condes
Santiago de Chile, Chile
P/F +56 2334 3074
Amayna Winery
Photos: © Antonio Corcuera

Curiosity
2-13-16, Tomigaya, Shibuya
151-0063 Tokyo, Japan
P +81 3 5452 0095
F +81 3 5454 9691
info@curiosity.jp
www.curiosity.jp
C-2
Photos: © Gwenael Nicolas

Delugan Meissl Associated Architects
Mittersteig 13/4
1040 Vienna, Austria
P +43 1585 3690
F +43 1585 3690 11
office@deluganmeissl.at
www.deluganmeissl.at
Haus Ray 1
Photos: © Hertha Hurnaus/Rupert Steiner

Drozdov & Partners
Ul. Darvina 31, of.1
61002 Kharkov, Ukraine
P +38 057 7587 690
F +38 057 7587 691
office@drozdov-partners.com
www.drozdov-partners.com
"Yaske" Sushi Bar
Photos: © Andrey Avdeenko

EEA—Erick van Egeraat Associated Architects
Calandstraat 23
3016 CA Rotterdam, The Netherlands
P +31 10 436 9686
F +31 10 436 9573
eea.nl@eea-architects.com
www.eea-architects.com
Popstage Mezz Breda
Photos: © Christian Richters

EMBT—Enric Miralles & Benedetta Tagliabue
Pasaje de la Paz 10 bis, principal
08002 Barcelona, Spain
P +34 93 412 53 42
publicacio@mirallestagliabue.com
www.mirallestagliabue.com
Scottish Parliament
Photos: © Duccio Malagamba
Sta. Caterina Market
Photos: © Duccio Malagamba

Emmanuel Combarel Dominique Marrec Architectes
7 Passage Turquetil
75011 Paris, France
P +33 1 4493 2060
F +33 1 4493 2061
www.combarel-marrec.com
Lycée La Tourelle Gymnasium
Photos: © Nouveau Dossier/Philippe Ruault

Enric Ruiz-Geli
Pasaje Mercader 10, bajos 3.ª
08008 Barcelona, Spain
P +34 93 215 05 53
F +34 93 215 78 74
Villa Bio
Photos: © Luis Ros

Estudio Lamela Arquitectos
C/O'Donnell 34
28009 Madrid, Spain
P +34 91 574 36 00
F +34 91 574 44 79
lamela@lamela.com
www.lamela.com
New Aerial Terminal at Madrid-Barajas Airport
Photos: © Manuel Renau

Fasch & Fuchs
Stumpergasse 14/25 im Hof
1060 Vienna, Austria
P +43 1597 3532
F +43 1597 3532 99
office@faschundfuchs.com
www.faschundfuchs.com
Kindermuseum
Photos: © Paul Ott

Future Systems
20 Victoria Gardens
W11 3PE London, UK
P +44 207 243 7670
F +44 207 243 7690
email@future-systems.com
www.future-systems.com
Selfridges
Photos: © Richard Davies

Fxfowle Architects
22 West 19 Street
New York, NY 10011, USA
P +1 21 2627 1700
F +1 21 2463 8716
info@fxfowle.com
www.fxfowle.com
Stillwell Avenue Terminal
Photos: © John Bartelstone

Gehry Partners
12541 Beatrice Street
Los Angeles, CA 90066, USA
www.foga.com
Hotel Marqués de Riscal, The Luxury Collection
Photos: © Adrian Tyler
Marta Museum
Photos: © Thomas Mayer

Germán del Sol
Camino de las Flores 11441, Las Condes
Santiago de Chile, Chile
P +56 2214 1214
F +56 2214 1147
contacto@germandelsol.cl
www.germandelsol.cl
Remota Hotel
Photos: © Felipe Camus

GMP Architekten
Hardenbergstraße 4-5
10623 Berlin, Germany
P +49 30 617 85 5
F +49 30 617 85 601
www.gmp-architekten.de
Berlin Central Station
Photos: © Marcus Bredt

Griffin Enright Architects
12468 Washington Blvd.
Los Angeles, CA 90066, USA
P +1 31 0391 4484
F +1 31 0391 4495
www.griffinenrightarchitects.com
Benedict Canyon Residence
Photos: © Benny Chan
The John Thomas Dye School
Photos: © Art Gray

Grimshaw
1 Conway Street
Fitzroy Square
London W1T 6LR, UK
P +44 207 291 4103
F +44 207 291 4194
www.grimshaw-architects.com
Frankfurt Trade Fair Hall
Photos: © Fotodesign Waltraud Krase
Southern Cross Station
Photos: © Shannon McGrath

Harmer Architecture Pty Ltd.
25 Budd Street, Collingwood
VIC 3066, Australia
P +61 3 9416 4466
F +61 3 9415 6110
www.harmer.com.au
Gatehouse Mausoleum, Melbourne General Cemetery
Photos: © Trevor Mein

Ingenhoven Architekten
Plange Mühle 1
D-40221 Düsseldorf, Germany
P +49 2113 010101
F +49 2113 010131
info@ingenhovenarchitekten.de
www.ingenhovenarchitekten.de
Peek & Cloppenburg Department Store (Chemnitz)
Photos: © H.G.Esch
Peek & Cloppenburg Department Store (Lübeck)
Photos: © H.G.Esch

Jarmund & Vigsnæs
Hausmanngate 6
0186 Oslo, Norway
P +47 22 994343
F +47 22 994353
jva@jva.no
www.jva.no
Svalbard Science Center
Photos: © Nils Petter Dale

John Portman & Associates Inc.
303 Peachtree Street, NE, Suite 4600
Atlanta, GA 30308, USA
P +1 40 4614 5555
F +1 40 4614 5553
info@portmanusa.com
www.portmanusa.com
Charles H. Jones Building at Macon State College
Photos: © Michael Portman, Matthew Skarr
Gwinnett University Center
Photos: © Michael Portman

Josep Llinàs i Carmona
Av. República Argentina 74, entlo.
08023 Barcelona, Spain
P +34 93 213 10 98
F +34 93 285 53 69
Jaume Fuster Public Library
Photos: © Duccio Malagamba

Josep Miàs i Gifre
C/Sant Cristòfol 12, bajos
08002 Barcelona, Spain
P +34 93 238 82 08
F +34 93 238 82 09
www.josepmias.com
Golf Club Fontanals
Photos: © Duccio Malagamba

Jun Itami Architect a Research Institute
Hanegi Museum 2-26-2, Hanegi, Setagaya-ku
Tokyo 156-0042, Japan
P +81 3 3325 1831
F +81 3 3325 3715
info@junitami.com
www.junitami.com
Podo Hotel
Photos: © Shigeyuki Morishita
Water Art Museum
Photos: © Shinichi Sato

Justo García Rubio
C/Obispo Segura Sáez 15, 4.º B
10001 Cáceres, Spain
www.justogarcia.com
Bus Station
Photos: © Hisao Suzuki

Kiessler & Partner Architekten Gmbh
Mauerkircherstraße 41
81679 Munich, Germany
P +49 89 987678
F +49 89 9810231
arch@kiessler.de
www.kiessler.de
K21 Düsseldorf
Photos: © Thomas Mayer

Kisho Kurokawa Architect & Associates
11th floor Aoyama Building
1-2-3 Kita Aoyama, Minato-ku
Tokyo 107-0061, Japan
P +81 3 3404 3481
F +81 3 3404 6222
kurokawa@kisho.co.jp
www.kisho.co.jp
Oita Main Stadium
Photos: © Koji Kobayashi

Luca Gazzaniga Architetti
Piazza Franscini 1
CH 6900 Lugano, Switzerland
P +41 91 972 10 69
F +41 91 972 10 41
studio@lucagazzaniga.com
www.lucagazzaniga.com
Cedrini House
Photos: © Ramak Fazel

Machné Architekten
Anichstrasse 4
6020 Innsbruck, Austria
P +43 5 1256 7631
F +43 5 1256 7645
office.ibk@machne.at
www.machne.at
Sarrasine
Photos: © Paul Ott

Marc Prosman Architecten BV
Overtoom 197
1054 HT Amsterdam, The Netherlands
P +31 20 489 2099
F +31 20 489 3658
architecten@prosman.nl
www.prosman.nl
Horse Barn
Photos: © Christian Richters

Mass Studies
Fuji Bldg. 4F
683-140 Hannam 2-dong Yongsan-gu
Seoul 140-892, South Korea
P +82 (0) 2 790 6528 9
F +82 (0) 2 790 6438
office@massstudies.com
www.massstudies.com
Pixel House
Photos: © Yong-Kwan Kim

Massimiliano Fuksas
Piazza del Monte di Pietà 30
00186 Rome, Italy
P +39 06 6880 7871
F +39 06 6880 7872
fuksaspublications@fuksas.it
www.fuksas.it
Europark 2
Photos: © Angelo Kaunat
New Trade Fair Milan
Photos: © Ruault, Archivio Fuksas, Paolo Riolzi

Monika Gora
Vilebovägen 4A
SE-217 63 Malmö, Sweden
P +46 40 911913
F +46 40 911903
info@gora.se
www.gora.se
The Glass Bubble
Photos: © Åke E:son Lindman

Nande Korpnik
Krekov Trg. 8
3000 Celje, Slovenia
P +386 34 926 086
F +386 34 926 087
Maksimilijan
Photos: © Miran Kambič

Neutelings Riedijk
PO Box 527
NL-3000 AM Rotterdam, The Netherlands
P +31 10 404 6677
F +31 10 414 2712
info@neutelings-riedijk.com
www.neutelings-riedijk.com
Housing Lakeshore Zone, Sphinxcn
Photos: © Jeroen Musch
Müllerpier, Block 3
Photos: © Daria Scagliola

Nolaster
C/Conde de Peñalver 92
28006 Madrid, Spain
P/F +34 91 401 61 57
oficina@nolaster.com
www.nolaster.com
OS House
Photos: © José Hevia

Nurmela-Raimoranta-Tasa
Kalevankatu 31
00100 Helsinki, Finland
P +358 96 866780
F +358 96 857588
www.n-r-t.fi
Moby Dick House
Photos: © Jussi Tiainen, Jyriki Tasa

Odden Rodrigues Architects
267 Stirling Highway
6010 Claremont, Western Australia
P +61 8 9383 3111
F +61 8 9385 2439
ora@iinet.net.au
Ozone Parade House
Photos: © Robert Frith/Acorn Photo Agency

ONL—Oosterhuis-Lénárd
Essenburgsingel 94c
3022 EG Rotterdam, The Netherlands
P +31 10 244 7039
F +31 10 244 7041
info@oosterhuis.nl
www.oosterhuis.nl
Cockpit Building
Photos: © ONL, Jeroen Bos

Original Vision Limited/Adrian McCarroll
4/F China Hong Kong Tower, 8 Hennessy Road
Wanchai, Hong Kong, China
P +852 2810 9797
F +852 2810 9790
www.original-vision.com
Samsara
Photos: © Andrzej Wronkowski/AFW Photo

Paulo David
Rua de Carreira 73, 5.º
042 Funchal, Portugal
P +351 291 281 840
F +351 291 281 852
Casa das Mudas Art Center
Photos: © FG + SG

Peter Cook, Coulin Fournier
P +43 189 00049
F +43 189 00049 15
mail@jonkhans.com
Art Museum Graz
Photos: © Paul Ott

Pittino & Ortner Architekturbüro
Holleneggerstrasse 6 A
8530 Deutschlandsberg, Austria
P +43 3462 70100
F +43 3462 701020
info@pittino-ortner.at
www.pittino-ortner.at
Public Bath Wellenbad Gleisdorf
Photos: © Paul Ott

Plan 01 Architects
89 Rue de Reuilly
75012 Paris, France
P +33 1 5333 2410
F +33 1 5333 2411
contact@plan01.com
www.plan01.com
Historical Museum of Vendée
Photos: © Stéphane Chalmeau, Frédéric Delangle

Purpur Architektur
Brockmanngasse 5
8010 Graz, Austria
www.purpur.cc
Mur Insel
Photos: © Paul Ott

Renzo Piano Building Workshop
Via P. Paolo Rubens 29
16158 Genoa, Italy
P +39 01 0617 11
F +39 01 0617 1350
italy@rpbw.com
www.rpbw.com
Padre Pio Pilgrimage Church
Photos: © Michel Denancé, Gianni Berengo Gardin

Richard Rogers Partnership
Thames Wharf
Rainville Road
W6 9HA London, UK
P +44 207 385 1235
F +44 207 385 8409
www.richardrogers.co.uk
Hesperia Tower Hotel
Photos: © David Cardelús, Pedro Pegenaute
Minami Yamashiro Primary School
Photos: © Katsuhisa Kida
New Aerial Terminal at Madrid-Barajas Airport
Photos: © Manuel Renau

RKW Architektur & Städtebau
Tersteegenstraße 30
40474 Düsseldorf, Germany
P +49 2114 3670
F +49 2114 367111
info@rkwmail.de
www.rkw-as.de
Audi Electronic Center
Photos: © Bernd Nöhrig
House of the Medical Fraternity
Photos: © Ansgar van Treeck, Michael Reisch

Salmela Architect
630 West 4th Street
Duluth, MN 55806, USA
P +1 21 8724 7517
F +1 21 8728 6805
ddsalmela@charter.net
www.salmelaarchitect.com
Emerson Sauna
Photos: © Peter Bastianelli Kerze

Sauerbruch Hutton Architects
Lehrterstraße 57
10557 Berlin, Germany
P +49 3039 78210
F +49 3039 782130
office@sauerbruchhutton.com
www.sauerbruchhutton.com
Experimental Factory
Photos: © Geritt Engel

Shuhei Endo Architect Institute
5-15-11 Nishitenma, Kita-ku
530-0047 Osaka, Japan
P +81 6 6312 7455
F +81 6 6312 7456
endo@paramodern.com
www.paramodern.com
Rooftecture S
Photos: © Yoshiharu Matsumura
Springtecture B
Photos: © Yoshiharu Matsumura

Slade Architecture
150 Broadway 807
New York, NY 10038, USA
P + 1 212 677 6380
F + 1 212 677 6330
Info@sladearch.com
www.sladearch.com
Pixel House
Photos: © Yong-Kwan Kim

Smarch, Mathys & Stücheli Architekten
Neuengasse 41
3011 Bern, Switzerland
P +41 31 312 9600
F +41 31 312 9601
www.smarch.ch
New Apostolic Church
Photos: © Thomas Jantscher
Wave of Bern
Photos: © Dominique Uldry

Spacelab
404 Kingswharf
301 Kingsland Road
E8 4ds, London, UK
P +44 207 684 5392
F +44 207 684 5393
info@spacelab.co.uk
www.spacelab.co.uk
Great Ormond Street Hospital
Photos: © Jefferson Smith

Stefan Sterf Architekten BDA
Fehrbellinerstraße 31
10119 Berlin, Germany
P +49 3028 098582
F +49 3028 27411
sterfarchitekten@t-online.de
Sunny Side Up
Photos: © Isabella Scheel

Steven Holl Architects
450 West 31st Street, 11th floor
New York, NY 10001, USA
P + 1 21 2629 7262
F + 1 21 2629 7312
mail@stevenholl.com
www.stevenholl.com
Turbulence House
Photos: © Paul Warchol
Whitney Water Purification Facility and Park
Photos: © Paul Warchol

Úrsula Heredia, Ramón Velasco
F +34 97 672 42 66
Roman Theatre
Photos: © Thomas Mayer

Vito Acconci
20 Jay Street, Suite #215
Brooklyn, New York, NY 11201, USA
studio@acconci.com
www.acconci.com
Mur Insel
Photos: © Paul Ott

Wilkinson Eyre Architects
24 Britton Street
EC1M 5UA London, UK
P +44 207 608 7900
F +44 207 608 7901
www.wilkinsoneyre.com
Davies Alpine House
Photos: © Helene Binet

© 2007 daab
cologne london new york

published and distributed worldwide by
daab gmbh
friesenstr. 50
d-50670 köln

p +49 - 221 - 913 927 0
f +49 - 221 - 913 927 20

mail@daab-online.com
www.daab-online.com

publisher ralf daab
rdaab@daab-online.com

creative director feyyaz
mail@feyyaz.com

editorial project by loft publications
© 2007 loft publications

editor and texts sergi costa duran

layout anabel naranjo
english translation jay noden
german translation susanne engler
french translation catherine collin
italian translation barbara burani

printed in china

isbn 978-3-937718-61-3